At the Top of Their Game

# Drew Brees

## Record-Breaking Quarterback

Gerry Boehme

Cavendish Square
New York

Published in 2020 by Cavendish Square Publishing, LLC
243 5th Avenue, Suite 136, New York, NY 10016



First Edition



Library of Congress Cataloging-in-Publication Data

Names: Boehme, Gerry, author.
Title: Drew Brees : record-breaking quarterback / Gerry Boehme.
Description: First edition. | New York : Cavendish Square, 2020. | Series: At the top of their game | Audience: Grade 9 to 12. | Includes bibliographical references and index.
Identifiers: LCCN 2019013492 (print) | LCCN 2019016438 (ebook) | ISBN 9781502651235 (ebook) | ISBN 9781502651228 (library bound) | ISBN 9781502651204 (pbk.) | ISBN 9781502651211 (6 pack)
Subjects: LCSH: Brees, Drew, 1979- —Juvenile literature. | Football players—United States—Biography—Juvenile literature. | Quarterbacks (Football)—United States—Biography—Juvenile literature.
Classification: LCC GV939.B695 (ebook) | LCC GV939.B695 B65 2020 (print) | DDC 796.332092 [B] —dc23
LC record available at https://lccn.loc.gov/2019013492

Editor: Jodyanne Benson
Copy Editor: Michele Suchomel-Casey
Associate Art Director: Alan Sliwinski
Designer: Joe Parenteau
Production Coordinator: Karol Szymczuk
Photo Research: J8 Media

The photographs in this book are used by permission and through the courtesy of: Cover, pp. 4, 90 Chris Graythen/Getty Images; pp. 8, 24–25, 32, 41, 54, 62, 71, 78 ©AP Images; p. 10 Scott Cunningham/Getty Images; pp. 14–15 Douglas Jones/Icon SMI/Newscom; p. 16 Tyler Kaufman/Getty Images; p. 21 Mark Cunningham/Getty Images; p. 28 Icon Sportswire/Getty Images; p. 34 Sandra Dukes/WireImage/Getty Images; pp. 36–37 Marsha Williamson Mohr/Alamy Stock Photo; p. 44 Peter Brouillet/Getty Images; p. 50 Al Tielemans/Sports Illustrated/Getty Images; pp. 56–57 Brian Nolan/Shutterstock.com; pp. 60–61 Bloomberg/Getty Images; pp. 64–65, 84–85 Bob Rosato/Sports Illustrated/Getty Images; pp. 68, 86 ZUMA/Alamy Stock Photo; p. 82 Win McNamee/Getty Images; p. 94 Josh Brasted/Getty Images; p. 96 Chip Somodevilla/Getty Images.

Printed in the United States of America

At the Top of Their Game

## Contents

Introduction

# A Star On and Off the Field

Drew Brees is a great football player. A star quarterback for many years in the National Football League (NFL), Brees has thrown for more yards, more completions, and more touchdowns than any other player in league history as of 2019. Brees has been chosen for more than ten Pro Bowls, and, as of 2019, he has twice won NFL Offensive Player of the Year.

In perhaps his greatest achievement, Drew Brees led his New Orleans Saints teammates to their first and only NFL championship, winning Super Bowl XLIV after the 2009 season. Not surprisingly, Brees capped his performance by winning the Super Bowl's Most Valuable Player (MVP) Award.

The Drew Brees story extends far beyond on-field heroics, however. Brees has overcome personal adversity to help redefine what it means to be a successful quarterback in today's NFL, and he has helped revolutionize football's offensive strategy. Even more impressively, Brees has used his fame to become a role model and dedicate much of his life to helping those in need.

*Opposite:* Quarterback Drew Brees kisses the Vince Lombardi Trophy after leading his New Orleans Saints to the Super Bowl XLIV championship on February 7, 2010.

## Setting the Standard

Some have described playing quarterback in the NFL as the most difficult job in sports. Quarterbacks need to be athletic, of course, with powerful, accurate arms and a quick release. They require enough speed to avoid pass rushers, gain yards, and make plays. Quarterbacks also need to be intelligent and poised, calm yet competitive, and able to function effectively under intense scrutiny and pressure.

Size has always been an important factor in judging a quarterback's potential. From the time 6-foot (1.8 meters) Drew Brees first stepped on a football field, many considered him to be too short to become an elite quarterback. Brees, however, proved them wrong at every level, setting records and winning championships in high school, college, and professional football. Brees's success helped pave the way for other "short" quarterbacks like Russell Wilson to be drafted and star in the NFL.

## Facing Adversity

Drew Brees's climb to the top did not come easily. Brees overcame many setbacks along the way, including serious knee and shoulder injuries that could have ended his career. He also experienced deep personal loss when his mother suddenly passed away just before his Super Bowl season.

Brees rose to the challenge of leading poor teams to greatness. In fact, he did it three times. After Brees joined a losing program at Purdue University, they posted winning records and qualified for postseason bowl games in all four of Brees's college years.

Drafted into the NFL by the last place San Diego Chargers, Brees first led them to respectability, then to the top spot in their division and a playoff appearance. When he later signed as a free agent with the New Orleans Saints, Brees took them even farther, helping the team rise from the bottom of the NFL to a Super Bowl championship.

## Devotion to Service

The Drew Brees legacy encompasses much more than football, however, and his influence on the community extends well beyond the record book.

While he was still in high school, Brees decided to follow his faith and try to make life better for other people. Brees worked with many charities while attending Purdue University, and he remains involved with its community more than eighteen years after he graduated.

When Brees turned professional, he continued to devote much of his personal time to helping people, especially children, improve their lives. Working closely with his wife, Brittany, Brees established his own charitable organization, which is called the Brees Dream Foundation. It has now raised more than $25 million for worthy causes.

In recognition of his work on and off the field, Brees has received many honors and awards, including being named the NFL's Walter Payton Man of the Year. President Barack Obama also appointed Brees cochair of the President's Council on Fitness, Sports, and Nutrition.

Immediately after joining the Saints, Drew Brees took a hands-on role in helping to rebuild New Orleans after Hurricane Katrina devastated the city.

## Accepting the Challenge

Many people think that Drew Brees has performed his greatest charitable work right at home in New Orleans. When the Saints recruited Brees to join them as their quarterback, the city had not yet recovered from Hurricane Katrina's deadly impact. Brees witnessed Katrina's destructive effects before he decided to play for the Saints, and he made a commitment to help rebuild his new city as well as his team.

In the foreword for Drew Brees's book *Coming Back Stronger*, former teammate Mark Brunell called Brees a "modern-day hero" who brought hope as well as a football championship to New Orleans. His leadership and generosity have made him a role model for many. Today, Drew Brees continues to make a difference, both as an athlete and as a human being.

Chapter 1

# A Born Athlete

Drew Brees was destined to be a great football player and began his steady climb to stardom at an early age. He was raised in Texas by an athletic family. Football is very popular in Texas, but the passion extends far beyond professional or college teams. High school football reigns supreme across the entire state. As depicted in the book, movie, and television series *Friday Night Lights,* Friday night is also called "football night" in most Texas towns. Streets often look deserted as Texans gather at the local high school football field to watch their team play long-time rivals, with the season's bragging rights at stake. Craig Hlavaty wrote in the *Houston Chronicle,* "High school football exists in other states, but in Texas it has grown to be a widescreen spectacle. It's mythic."

*Opposite:* Drew Brees uses the birthmark on his cheek to show that all people have unique and special qualities.

## Son of Athletes

Drew Christopher Brees was born in Austin, Texas, on January 15, 1979. The city of Austin serves as the state capital and is famous for its cultural activities, restaurants, and music, but it is also a big sports town. The University of Texas claims Austin as its home, and its football games routinely attract more than 100,000 fans to Darrell K. Royal–Texas Memorial Stadium.

Both of Drew's parents were lawyers, but they had also been great athletes. His father, Eugene Wilson "Chip" Brees, played college basketball at Texas A&M University. Drew's mother, Mina Ruth Brees, may have been even more skilled. In high school, Mina excelled in track, volleyball, and basketball, and she was an accomplished tennis player.

If Mina Ruth was growing up today, she probably would have received many college scholarship offers when she graduated high school. Unfortunately, back in the late 1960s, women did not receive as many opportunities for athletic scholarships as men. Mina still managed to become one of the first women to attend Texas A&M University, which had previously been an all-male military school. Mina and Chip first met when they both attended Texas A&M.

## Distinctive Mark

Drew Brees was born with a large birthmark on his cheek. As a child, Drew's parents told him that the mark had been left by angels who kissed him on his face, but some classmates still teased him about it.

Drew's parents considered trying to have the blemish removed, but they chose not to take any action until their son got older.

Drew later decided to take pride in his birthmark, feeling that it made him stand out from other people. Years later, as Brees rose to fame in the NFL, his fans drew similar marks on their own cheeks to honor him.

## Football Genes

Looking at Brees's family background, it can be said that football is part of Drew's DNA. His grandfather Ray Akins, Mina's father, served as a marine in World War II. Ray then became one of the most successful high school football coaches in Texas state history, winning 302 games across 38 years. After retiring in 1988, Ray was inducted into the Texas Sports Hall of Fame in 1992.

Ray's son Marty, Mina's brother and Drew's uncle, played quarterback for the University of Texas and was named All-Southwest Conference in 1975. Marty was later drafted by the NFL, but he retired after two years to become a lawyer. Marty was inducted into the Texas Sports Hall of Fame in 1987, making him and Ray the only father and son to earn that honor.

## Close Siblings

Growing up, Drew played football and baseball with his brother Reid, who was two years younger. No matter what sport or game Drew tried, he always played to win. Many people thought that Drew inherited his competitive nature from his mother, whom he has described as very competitive.

While they played hard against each other, Drew and Reid were friends as well as brothers. Their relationship helped get them through a very difficult time shortly after their family moved from Austin to Westlake, an upscale suburb of Fort Worth, Texas.

YLOR

Drew Brees's younger brother Reid helped lead Baylor University to the College Baseball World Series.

## Family Split

Chip and Mina Brees had a difficult relationship, and Drew and Reid often found themselves caught in the middle of their disagreements. Their parents decided to end their marriage when Drew was only seven and Reid was five. Brees recalls that his parents' divorce did

Drew Brees's grandfather Ray Akins (*center*) and uncle Marty Akins (*right*) were both elected to the Texas Sports Hall of Fame.

not go smoothly, leaving both sides with bitter feelings. Drew took the breakup hard and often cried himself to sleep.

Drew and his brother now spent their time in two different homes, alternating days or weekends with each parent. Luckily, Drew and Reid had each other, and in some ways, their parents' divorce helped them grow even closer.

It also helped that their grandfather, Ray Akins, still coached high school football at that time, and Drew and Reid spent summers on his ranch. When their grandfather left each day to conduct summer practice, the brothers regularly tagged along. Drew and Reid brought water to the players, retrieved loose balls, and helped move equipment around the field. Brees remembers, "We'd be over there, me and my brother … tossing the ball on the side and just thought that was the greatest thing ever, being a part of that and watching grandpa coach and going to his games."

## Early Signs

The more that Drew saw football, the more he liked it. Two of his heroes were NFL quarterbacks—Joe Montana and Drew Bledsoe. Joe Montana had gained fame as one of the most successful quarterbacks in league history, leading his San Francisco 49ers to four Super Bowl championships. Drew Bledsoe had led his New England Patriots to two Super Bowl appearances, and Brees also liked the fact that they shared the same first name.

As Brees grew up, people began to notice that he was, simply put, a great athlete. Sports helped him to deal with his parents' divorce, and he soon showed off his skills. Just before Drew entered the sixth grade, his mother insisted that he leave the public school system to attend the private St. Andrew's Episcopal School, where she thought Drew would receive a solid education as well as face tougher athletic competition.

Drew first started playing organized football while at St. Andrew's, but he did not play the physical version that included tackling the ball carrier to the ground. St. Andrew's offered only flag football, where defenders stop the ball carrier by pulling a marker, or flag, from the player's belt. While flag and tackle football require many of the same skills, flag football stresses throwing, catching, and running rather than blocking and hard physical contact.

## All-Around Athlete

While Drew liked football, he and Reid also played many other sports, including baseball and tennis. Drew truly loved baseball, and at one point, he considered giving up football to concentrate on baseball. Reid focused on baseball, and he later received a college scholarship to Baylor University, in Waco, Texas. Reid then helped his team reach the College World Series in Omaha, Nebraska, in 2005. Drew later said that "Watching my brother play in Omaha in 2005 ranks up there as one of the proudest moments in my life."

Drew also became an outstanding tennis player. His mother played on the Austin city championship tennis team and always defeated her son on the courts, which bothered him quite a bit. Drew had better success against his peers, however, and by age twelve, he had advanced to rank first in Texas and third in the nation in his age group. Brees's early tennis rivals included Andy Roddick, who went on to become one of the top tennis players in the world. Brees defeated Roddick several times, but he decided to give up tennis when he was thirteen.

## New Challenge

Looking for better academic and athletic programs after middle school, Mina enrolled Drew in Westlake High School, on the west side of Austin, which was in a different district. When Drew entered as a freshman, he did not know anyone on the football team. Many of the students had already played tackle football together in middle school. It also turned out that another freshman, Johnny Rodgers, was the younger brother of the varsity team's starting quarterback. Johnny already had been groomed to start at quarterback for the freshman team.

Luckily, Westlake had two first-year teams, and Drew had developed his quarterback skills while playing flag football for St. Andrew's. Drew won the starting job for the Westlake freshman "B" team, and he led his teammates to an undefeated season. The next year, however, Drew found himself on the bench as Johnny Rodgers took the starting role as quarterback of the junior varsity team.

Fearing that he would never get the chance to play, Drew considered quitting football and concentrating on baseball. His mother convinced him to be patient and wait for his opportunity. After considering her advice and the success that his grandfather and uncle had experienced, Drew agreed to give football another chance.

## Taking Advantage

Just one week later, Johnny Rodgers suffered a serious knee injury in the final practice game before the regular season began. Rodgers would miss the entire year, and Drew Brees now became the starting quarterback for the Westlake junior varsity team. Drew had received his opportunity, and he would not disappoint.

Drew opened the season by completing 9 of 10 passes for 315 yards and 4 touchdowns. After Drew led the team to ten victories and an undefeated season, his coach Ron Schroeder said that Drew might not have had the chance if Johnny Rodgers had not been injured. When Johnny returned the next year, he took note of Drew's talent and leadership. Johnny switched positions to defensive safety for the good of the team.

## Setback

Drew took the reins as starting quarterback for the Westlake varsity team during his junior year, and he once again led the team to an undefeated season as well as a spot in the Texas state high school playoffs. After winning their first two playoff games, however, Drew suffered his own devastating knee injury in December 1995, tearing his left anterior cruciate ligament (ACL) during the second quarter. Drew returned to the sidelines on crutches to watch his team rally from behind to win. With Drew no longer able to play, however, Westlake lost in the next round to the eventual state champions.

During his junior year, Drew had led his varsity team to twelve wins, no losses, and one tie. Drew had not lost a game in his entire high school career, but his serious knee injury now cast a shadow on his future, especially his prospects for attracting college scholarship offers.

## College Concerns

While colleges often scout major high school talent from the time they enter as freshmen, many athletes prove themselves ready for the next big stage while they are juniors. The summer before senior year also features large football camps, where high school players get the

An all-around athlete, Drew Brees also played baseball and tennis before deciding to concentrate on football in high school.

chance to showcase their skills and attract college attention. Players who excel often receive scholarship offers and commit to their future college teams well before they graduate high school.

College coaches can only offer a limited number of scholarships and spots on the team, and they face enormous pressure to recruit the right players to make them successful. Players experience similar stress. Some non-scholarship players still manage to make their college teams as "walk-ons" and receive financial aid afterwards, but that path is tremendously difficult and risky. Most high school players work hard to attract scholarship offers in advance, along with the attention of the college coaching staff.

While many colleges had already expressed interest in recruiting Drew to play quarterback for them, some had doubts about his height and weight. Drew was 6 feet (1.8 m) tall and weighed 180 pounds (82 kilograms), and some coaches felt he was too short and light to successfully quarterback a major college team. Drew's father, Chip, explained, "I think sometimes recruiters do get in this mold mentality. If you have a boy [who fits the typical profile], the recruiter can never be criticized for taking that kid, even if he doesn't work out, because he fit the mold. But if a coach takes a chance on a kid who doesn't fit the mold, now he's leaving himself open to criticism."

## Offers Fade

Now Drew needed major knee surgery. Many colleges wondered if he could regain his skill and strength or whether he would even return at all. Those doubts scared off two major colleges that Drew was strongly interested in: the University of Texas and Texas A&M.

"All the letters stopped," Drew remembers. He had hoped for baseball scholarship offers as well, but those also slowed.

Looking back, Drew Brees now describes his high school injury as a defining moment in his life. He'd seen some of his friends experience similar injuries, and some couldn't recover their speed or mobility. The thought of a torn ACL was "devastating to me," Drew remembers, "because I thought I might be in the same boat as them."

## Faith and Recovery

Drew recalls a time shortly after his injury when he was sitting in church, questioning whether he could continue with sports and what he should do with his life. According to Drew, "The minister was saying that God was looking for a few good men to carry the torch and represent the Christian faith, and I just remember thinking to myself [that] I'd like to be one of those few good men." Drew decided to devote himself to the Christian faith and use it to help him make decisions in his life from that time on. "I made a decision not to let something negative control my emotions."

Drew found a local high school football coach, Carment Kiara, to help plan his rehabilitation. After spending months using crutches, Drew worked for six months to restore strength in his knee and improve his overall conditioning. He even built up muscle and increased his weight to 195 pounds (89 kg). Carament Kiara later said that Drew "never doubted. He's a doer."

Drew returned to play quarterback for Westlake during his senior year in 1996. He once again led his team to an undefeated regular season. This time, Drew and his teammates completed their mission by sweeping through the playoffs, finishing the season with sixteen victories and no losses and winning the

Texas state championship. Drew threw for 31 touchdowns and 3,528 yards in his senior year, and he won the Texas High School Football Most Valuable Player (MVP) Award. Drew never lost a game as a high school quarterback.

## Doubt Remains

During Drew's senior year, his parents aggressively reached out to colleges and sent them highlight tapes of his games. Drew's outstanding senior season did rekindle some interest. While schools liked his football sense and his quickness, many still wondered if Drew had the size and strength to be an effective college quarterback. "I was a skinny, runt-looking kid," Drew said, and "I wouldn't have [wanted] me either."

The fact that the University of Texas did not pursue Drew also concerned many other colleges. Drew played in Austin, home to the Longhorns. The university could watch him every week, while other colleges had to rely on game films or just a few live performances. Some teams thought that if Texas didn't recruit Drew, maybe they

Drew Brees quarterbacked his high school team to the Texas state championship and was chosen MVP.

shouldn't either. Westlake High School offensive coordinator Neal Lahue remembers, "We told them he was the most accurate passer we had ever seen, that he was a great leader and a tough kid. Nobody listened."

## A Big Fan

One college coach, however, strongly believed in Drew Brees. Joe Tiller was head football coach at the University of Wyoming when he first started to recruit Drew. Tiller then moved to the Purdue University Boilermakers as their head coach, and he still wanted Drew. Tiller loved the fact that Drew would not let mistakes get the better of him. "He would quickly move on to the next play ... If you are thinking about the last play, you'll never execute the next play," Tiller said.

In the end, Drew did receive several college scholarship offers. He narrowed his choices to two major universities: Purdue University and the University of Kentucky. Coach Hal Mumme had just arrived at Kentucky, so he and Joe Tiller needed to put together their new teams very quickly. Both coaches also used offenses that relied on passing, and they needed great quarterbacks.

Kentucky already had a high-level quarterback, Tim Couch, who would later become a Heisman Trophy candidate (an award for the top college player) and play in the NFL. Purdue had developed many great quarterbacks in their past, including NFL stars Len Dawson and Bob Griese. However, the Boilermakers did not currently have a star quarterback, and Joe Tiller thought that Drew Brees fit the bill.

## Off to Indiana

Drew decided to accept Purdue's scholarship offer. He later admitted that he had no idea where the university was located when they first contacted him. Based in West Lafayette, Indiana, the Boilermakers played in the powerful Big Ten Conference.

That was very important to Drew because many college football experts believed that the Big Ten was college football's best conference.

In the past, Purdue had ranked as one of the Big Ten's strongest teams. When Drew arrived on campus in 1997, however, Purdue's football program was struggling. They had managed only one winning season in the previous sixteen years. Coach Tiller intended to instill a new culture and attitude, and he planned to use a high-powered offense with Drew as its leader.

## Patience

Tiller did not want to start Drew before he was ready, however. College can be very different than high school. Players often find themselves living away from home for the first time. The academic requirements are often tougher, players are bigger and stronger, and games feature more pressure and attract more attention, sometimes on a national scale. Drew Brees would have to wait a bit before he became a college football star.

15

Chapter 2

# Preparing for Greatness

When coach Joe Tiller arrived at Purdue University, he installed what is called a "spread offense," which features more passes than runs and uses many wide receivers to "spread" the other team's defense across the entire field. Tiller believed that Brees's quickness and passing ability fit perfectly with his new offensive scheme, but he also wanted to give Brees time to transfer his skills from the practice field to an actual game.

## Waiting His Turn

In the fall of 1997, Drew Brees began his freshman year as number two on the depth chart behind starter and college senior Billy Dickens. Many coaches back then preferred that first-year players watch and learn from their older teammates before they played themselves. Brees felt fortunate that he appeared in eight games, even if his playing time usually came after the outcome had already been decided.

*Opposite:* Drew Brees set many college passing records as quarterback for the Purdue University Boilermakers.

Brees used that experience to learn Tiller's system and understand what it took to be a successful college quarterback. Even better, the Boilermakers were usually ahead when Brees took the field. Joe Tiller's first year at Purdue provided immediate and impressive results. After Purdue had gone 3–8 the previous season, Tiller's team won 9 games while losing only 3. Their season included an impressive postseason victory in the Alamo Bowl. Tiller's spread offense helped Billy Dickens throw for more than 3,000 yards and 21 touchdowns.

The Joe Tiller era had taken hold at Purdue, but it was going to need a new on-field general after Billy Dickens graduated. Understudy Drew Brees stood next in line to take over and direct the Boilermakers offense.

## Slow Start

Purdue's 1998 season opener took place on a national stage. The University of Southern California featured their own highly touted quarterback, freshman Carson Palmer. Palmer later went on to a successful NFL career. While Purdue lost 27–17, first-time starter Brees played well, passing for 2 touchdowns and completing 30 passes in 52 attempts.

Quickly recovering from their opening game disappointment, Brees and his Boilermakers won their next two games before traveling to South Bend, Indiana, to play perennial national football power Notre Dame. After leading much of the game, however, Brees threw two damaging interceptions, and Notre Dame came from behind to win in the final minute, 31–30.

Brees remarked later that he learned an important lesson against Notre Dame. No matter what the situation, he had to remain focused and in control. "We had the game won. All we had to do was get a first down or punt and let the defense do the rest ... It [the interception] was a bad decision on my part," he said later. Brees also realized, though, that he had played well for most of the game and that he could compete at a high level.

## Up and Down

The Boilermakers bounced back in their next game, soundly defeating unbeaten Minnesota 56–21. Brees completed 31 of 36 passes for 522 yards and 6 touchdowns. In his next game against tenth-ranked Wisconsin, Brees set a national record with 83 passing attempts and tied the record with 55 completions. He also threw four interceptions, however, and Purdue fell, 31–24. After another loss to Penn State, Brees's record as Purdue's starting quarterback had dropped to three wins and four losses.

## Winning Moves

The Penn State defeat turned out to be Purdue's final loss that season. Drew Brees and his team bounced back in a big way the next week, blowing out Illinois 42–9. The Boilermakers then rolled to the regular season finish line, winning their next four games to end at 8–4. The Boilermakers received another invitation to play in the Alamo Bowl—this time against Kansas State, the fourth-ranked team in the country. Brees then capped off his impressive sophomore year by throwing for three touchdowns. The last touchdown was thrown with fewer than 30 seconds remaining, and Purdue upset Kansas State 37–34.

During his first year as a college starting quarterback, Brees passed for six touchdowns in two different games.

Drew Brees threw for three touchdowns as Purdue upset heavily favored Kansas State in the 1998 Alamo Bowl.

Overall, Brees completed 361 passes for 3,983 total yards and 39 touchdowns, breaking school and Big Ten records in each category. After the season, Brees was named the Big Ten Offensive Player of the Year. Former Michigan State coach Nick Saban said that Brees reminded him of NFL quarterback Joe Montana, Brees's childhood idol.

Shortly after the Alamo Bowl, Brees had another experience that would change his life forever. While celebrating his twentieth birthday with friends on January 15, 1999, Brees met fellow Purdue student Brittany Dudchenko. After several more chance meetings, Drew and Brittany began dating. They eventually married in 2003.

## Starting Strong

The Boilermakers started strong in 1999. The team appointed Brees as offensive captain, and they won their first four games. Early in the season, Brees and wide receiver Vinny Sutherland teamed up for a 99-yard pass-and run, the longest play in Purdue history. The team soon slumped, however, and won only three more games. Purdue ended the season at 7–4 after losing the Outback Bowl in overtime to the Georgia Bulldogs.

Brees played well that season, throwing for 3,909 yards and 25 touchdowns. He also reduced his interceptions from the previous year. Brees also won many postseason honors; he was named first team Big Ten and second team All-American, and he finished fourth in the vote for the Heisman Trophy.

# Mentor and Partner

After playing college football as an offensive lineman at Montana State, Joe Tiller had a short professional career in the Canadian Football League (CFL) before joining the college coaching ranks in 1965. For the next twenty-five years, Tiller worked as an

Purdue coach Joe Tiller planned his offense to take advantage of Drew Brees's outstanding passing talent.

assistant coach at several schools, including Purdue University as defensive coordinator from 1983 to 1986. Tiller landed his first head-coaching job at Wyoming in 1991 and led them for six years, ending his run with a 10–2 record in his final season. Tiller then returned to Purdue as head coach in 1997.

When Tiller installed his spread offense at Purdue, his players moved so quickly that people began referring to their style as "basketball on grass." Tiller needed a great passing quarterback to run his offense, and he strongly felt that Drew Brees fit the bill. Working together, Brees and Tiller transformed the Big Ten Conference, breaking team and league passing records along the way. Brees's father, Chip, said that Drew "ended up in exactly the right place at exactly the right time."

Tiller coached at Purdue from 1997 to 2008, going 87–62 with only two losing seasons before he retired. When Tiller passed away in 2017, Brees fondly remembered his college mentor. "Coach Tiller was an important person in my life and to so many other guys who played for him," Brees said. "He did so much more than teach us how to win. He taught us life lessons and how to be great leaders and men."

Drew Brees excelled as a student at Purdue University, and he stayed involved in the local community after he graduated in 2001.

VERSITY
869

## Senior Raves

Many college players dream of someday joining the NFL, and Drew Brees was no exception. The NFL requires players to be out of high school at least three years before they become eligible for the NFL draft, and some college players choose to leave school after their junior year to pursue their professional career.

Drew Brees gave a lot of thought to leaving Purdue after his junior year. He had played well and won many awards. Brees thought he might be a high NFL draft pick, which could lead to a professional contract worth millions of dollars. After thinking it over, however, Brees decided to return to Purdue for his senior year. He said later that he and his team still had goals they had not accomplished.

The Purdue Boilermakers started the fall 2000 season ranked fifteenth in the country. They wound up winning the Big Ten cochampionship with a record of eight wins against four defeats. After leading a fourth-quarter comeback against Ohio State, Drew Brees was shocked to receive a telephone call from NFL star quarterback Peyton Manning, congratulating him on the victory. That was the first time Brees and Manning had spoken; it would not be the last.

As a reward for their successful season, Purdue University received an invitation to play in the Rose Bowl, which was their first invitation in thirty-four years. The Rose Bowl, which is college football's oldest and most prestigious postseason bowl game, matched the top teams from the Big Ten and the Pacific-12 (Pac-12) conferences.

While Purdue lost to the fourth-ranked University of Washington 34–24, Drew Brees once again put up stellar numbers for the season. He threw for 3,668 yards and 26 touchdowns, breaking the school scoring record, and he was again named the Big Ten's best offensive player. Brees also won the Maxwell Award for the top college player in the country, and he finished third in the Heisman voting.

## Shining Off the Field

More than just a football player, Drew Brees performed well in the classroom and on the athletic field. He attained a 3.42 GPA (grade point average) overall, including a perfect 4.0 during his spring 2000 semester. Brees also graduated in 2001 with honors from Purdue's Krannert School of Management, receiving his degree in Industrial Management. In recognition of his achievements, Brees was named an Academic All-American.

In addition to excelling as a student and a player, Drew Brees also volunteered his time with several charities. One of those charities was the Purdue Gentle Giants program, which helped elementary students who live near the university. He also volunteered with the American Lung Association, where he helped launch an antismoking program called "Enjoy the Brees." Other organizations that Brees volunteered with included the March of Dimes, the Muscular Dystrophy Association, the Boys and Girls Clubs, and the Boy Scouts of America.

## High Anxiety

While most college seniors typically wait to graduate before starting their careers, football players sometimes choose to finish school after the fall season to prepare for the NFL draft, which takes place the following April. It can be very busy and stressful time.

Players need to hire an agent to talk with NFL teams, consider offers, and negotiate contract terms. Players must also train for the NFL scouting combine, a week-long event held each February, where top-ranked college players go through a battery of intense drills, tests, and interviews that measure their skills, strength, intelligence, and personal makeup. Once that is done, college athletes face still more tests.

After the combine, major universities schedule their own Pro Days, where they invite NFL teams to come see their players demonstrate their skills. Some players also schedule private workouts for individual teams. A player who performs well can solidify his draft position and perhaps command a higher rookie salary. On the other hand, a bad showing can sabotage a player's chances to join the NFL, perhaps ending his professional dream despite a great college career.

## Different Path

Many NFL teams ranked Drew Brees second among all college quarterback prospects, behind Virginia Tech's Michael Vick. Brees passed for 2,000 more career yards than Vick and ran for nearly the same total yardage, but most NFL scouts thought that the taller, heavier, and faster Vick better fit the mold of an NFL quarterback.

Rather than leave school to train for the draft, Drew Brees chose to remain at Purdue to finish his degree and work out on his own. When Brees arrived at the combine, scouts once again questioned whether he was tall enough or strong enough to make it in the NFL. "People made such a big deal out of [my height]," Brees said at the time. "I just never believed that it mattered. To play the quarterback

Drew Brees joined the NFL as a rookie quarterback with the San Diego Chargers in 2001.

position, it's all in the heart and the mind." It did not help that Brees did not excel in the combine's passing drills.

In his favor, scouts noted that Brees had large hands, which helped him excel in baseball and basketball as well as football. He also showed impressive footwork, which helped him maintain his balance and throw the football powerfully and accurately. Brees had also shattered passing records while leading Purdue to three winning seasons, and he performed much better for NFL scouts during his private workouts after the combine.

## Draft Day

An NFL team's draft position depends on its record of wins and losses the previous season. The worst team gets the first choice in the draft. Other teams then take turns until the team with the best record drafts last. The teams then choose players in the same order during additional rounds.

The San Diego Chargers won only one game in 2000, so in April 2001 they held the number one draft choice. In many cases, teams with the first pick often try to sign a contract with the player they want before the draft officially begins.

The Chargers desperately needed a young quarterback, and they considered drafting Michael Vick. Vick, however, refused to negotiate a contract in advance. San Diego general manager John Butler then decided to trade his top pick to the Atlanta Falcons in return for multiple draft choices and an established player. The Falcons then drafted Vick number one.

## Charging Toward the NFL

Brees also believed that he would be chosen in the first round, but he was disappointed when no other team used their top pick to select a quarterback. When the second round of the draft began, San Diego again had the first choice. The Chargers had already drafted running back LaDainian Tomlinson, using the number five pick they received from Atlanta as part of their earlier trade. They still needed a quarterback, and Drew Brees remained available.

Using the first choice in the second round, the San Diego Chargers selected the record-setting passer from Purdue University to lead them to a better future. Drew Brees was headed to San Diego, California.

Riddell
9
21

Chapter 3

# Ascent, Recovery, and Revival

Drew Brees joined a struggling San Diego team that had lost more games than they won in every season since making the playoffs in 1995. The Chargers fell to a low point the previous year, winning only one game while losing fifteen. They knew they needed new on-field leadership, and they hoped that Drew Brees could provide it.

## Bench Time

Like many rookie quarterbacks, Brees would have to wait for his chance to shine. During his first year at Purdue, coach Joe Tiller sat Brees behind senior Billy Dickens. That allowed Brees to get comfortable with college football and campus life before facing the pressure of leading his team on the field. San Diego coach Mike Riley felt the same way. In those days, few NFL teams started rookie quarterbacks. They believed that NFL players were so skillful and the game plans so complex that young quarterbacks would be better served to sit behind a veteran for at least their first year. Brees would be no exception.

*Opposite:* Drew Brees made the Pro Bowl in his second year as San Diego's starting quarterback.

Instead, the Chargers signed veteran free agent Doug Flutie to start at quarterback for the 2001 season. They also wanted Flutie to mentor Brees. In many ways, the Chargers could not have made a better choice.

## Similar Story

At thirty-eight years old, Doug Flutie had found success in football, but it had not been an easy road. Flutie was even shorter than Brees, standing only 5 feet 10 inches (1.8 m) tall. Like Brees, Flutie had always been considered too small to play football. Even after starring in high school, Flutie received only one scholarship offer, from Boston College. He rewarded their faith by setting college records (since broken) for passing yards and total yards of offense. Flutie culminated his college career by winning the Heisman Trophy in 1984.

Despite his outstanding college performance, NFL teams still thought that Flutie was too short for the NFL. The Los Angeles Rams finally drafted him but only in the eleventh round. The Rams then traded Flutie to the Chicago Bears. Flutie played in the NFL until the New England Patriots released him after the 1989 season. Flutie went on to star in the Canadian Football League (CFL) for eight years, being named the league's outstanding player six times and winning three league championships. Flutie then returned to the NFL with the Buffalo Bills, making the Pro Bowl in 1998, before joining San Diego.

Doug Flutie and the Chargers started strong in Brees's rookie year, beginning the season with three consecutive victories. They won only twice after that, however, and they finished with five wins against eleven losses. Brees played in one game, completing 15 passes in 27 attempts, for 221 yards and one touchdown.

## New Leadership

After the season ended, the Chargers brought in a new coach to replace Mike Riley. Marty Schottenheimer had already worked with other great NFL quarterbacks, including Bernie Kosar with the Cleveland Browns and Joe Montana and Rich Gannon with the Kansas City Chiefs. In his first Chargers training camp, Schottenheimer held an open competition for starting quarterback. Brees played well and unseated Doug Flutie to claim the top spot for 2002. Flutie handled the transition with class and offered to help Brees in any way he could.

Brees and the Chargers began the 2002 season in impressive fashion. In his first NFL start, Brees completed 15 of 19 passes for 2 touchdowns, and San Diego defeated the Cincinnati Bengals 34–6. The Chargers went on to win their first four games and six of their first seven before hitting hard times. Brees and his team won only two more games and finished 8–8, missing the playoffs.

Drew Brees made some mistakes in his first year as a starter, but he still completed more than 60 percent of his passes and threw for 3,284 yards and 17 touchdowns. Unfortunately, Brees and his team would take a big step backward the next year.

## Tough Time

The Chargers lost their first five games to open the 2003 season. Brees did not play well; he was inconsistent and threw fifteen interceptions as he tried to do too much to help his losing team.

Midway through the year, Marty Schottenheimer replaced Brees as starting quarterback with Doug Flutie, now forty-one years old, but the spiral continued. With the season lost at 3–10, Schottenheimer started Brees for the last three games to evaluate him for the next year. While Brees played better than before, his team still lost two of their final three contests.

San Diego finished the season 4–12, the worst record in the league. Brees won only two of the eleven games he started, and his NFL future was in serious doubt. Due to their last place finish, the Chargers once again owned the number one pick in the upcoming NFL draft.

## Beyond the Field

While the 2003 season proved to be difficult, Brees still managed to look beyond football to try and make a difference in the lives of others. Continuing the work he had started in college, Brees devoted significant personal time to charitable work. Brees also married his college sweetheart, Brittany, in February. Later that year, Drew and Brittany founded the Brees Dream Foundation, a charity that raises money for various causes, such as helping cancer patients and providing educational opportunities for children and families.

## New Quarterbacks

Heading into the NFL draft in April 2004, football experts and fans alike speculated what San Diego would do with their number one draft pick. With every new college prospect at their doorstep, who would the Chargers select? San Diego needed help in many areas. Would they draft an aggressive defensive lineman or linebacker to stop the run and rush opposing passers, a swift wide receiver to stretch the defenses, or an offensive lineman to protect the quarterback and open holes for runners? Would San Diego give up on Drew Brees and select a new, young quarterback to lead them to a brighter future?

During his two seasons as a starter, Brees had thrown for more interceptions (thirty-one) than touchdowns (twenty-nine), and he had won only ten games while losing seventeen. Meanwhile, three elite college quarterbacks had risen to the top of NFL wish lists: Eli Manning from the University of Mississippi, Philip Rivers from North Carolina State, and Ben Roethlisberger from Miami University.

Given their doubts about Brees, the Chargers decided that they needed to draft one of the three quarterback prospects. They first targeted Manning, who was Peyton Manning's younger brother. Eli and his team made it clear, however, that he did not want to sign with the Chargers. San Diego drafted Manning anyway, while the New York Giants chose Philip Rivers with the fourth pick. The Chargers then quickly traded Manning to the Giants for Rivers, plus three other draft choices.

## Competition

The San Diego Chargers had clearly shown that they were no longer fully committed to Drew Brees as their starting quarterback. Neither Marty Schottenheimer nor new Chargers general manager A. H. Smith had drafted Brees. Schottenheimer had coached Philip Rivers in a college all-star game and liked him a lot. Rivers had a great arm and the size that NFL teams look for, standing at 6 feet 5 inches (2 m) and weighing 230 pounds (104 kg).

# Friendly Rivals

When legendary NFL quarterback Peyton Manning reached out to compliment Drew Brees while he was still at Purdue University, neither man could have predicted that Brees would soon join Manning in the NFL as a star quarterback.

Drew Brees (*left*) and Peyton Manning (*right*) rank as two of the greatest quarterbacks in NFL history.

Brees and Manning wound up facing each other five times. While Manning's team won three of four regular season games, Brees's Saints beat Manning's Colts in the greatest NFL showdown of all, the Super Bowl.

Drew Brees and Peyton Manning share many other fascinating connections. NFL star Archie Manning played quarterback for the Saints before settling in New Orleans after he retired. His sons, Peyton and Eli, then grew up in New Orleans before they, too, became elite NFL quarterbacks. Archie later helped Drew Brees relocate to New Orleans when he came to play quarterback for the Saints, and the two families became close.

When Peyton graduated from the University of Tennessee, he and Washington State quarterback Ryan Leaf ranked as the two top prospects in the draft. The Indianapolis Colts chose Manning, while the San Diego Chargers drafted Leaf. While Manning went on to greatness, Leaf failed badly, leaving the Chargers to struggle for years until they drafted Brees.

In October 2018, Brees broke Peyton Manning's NFL record for most career passing yards. Manning then posted a funny video congratulating his friend, including a photo of the two quarterbacks standing together in 2000. "Way to go. Proud of you," Manning said. "Good luck the rest of the way."

Brees now had to compete with Philip Rivers in summer training camp to see who would direct San Diego's offense that fall. As he had shown before, Drew Brees was up for the challenge. He would not let anyone take his job without a fight.

Brees hired dieticians, exercise experts, personal trainers, and even a former Major League Baseball pitching coach to help him improve his body and his passing technique. When training camp began in July 2004, Brees was ready. Meanwhile, Philip Rivers and the Chargers did not agree to contract terms until late August, and Brees took advantage. By opening day, Drew Brees had cemented his position as starting quarterback, with Doug Flutie as his backup and Philip Rivers listed as third-string.

## Big Turnaround

Brees played well to open the 2004 season as San Diego defeated the Houston Texans, 27–20. Brees did poorly as his team lost their next two games, however, and it looked like the Chargers might be headed toward a quarterback controversy. Brees quickly put that thought to rest.

Brees separated his left shoulder in the team's fourth game, but he remained on the field and led his Chargers to a dominant 38–17 win over the Tennessee Titans. That victory began a string of eleven wins in thirteen games, with the only losses coming by one point to Michael Vick's Atlanta Falcons and in overtime to Peyton Manning's Indianapolis Colts. The Chargers finished 12–4, rising from worst in the league to first place in their division and a playoff spot.

While San Diego lost their first-round postseason game to the New York Jets in overtime, Brees and the team still managed an incredible season. Brees completed more than 65 percent of his passes and threw for 3,159 yards, 27 touchdowns, and only 7 interceptions. In 2003, Brees ranked twenty-ninth among NFL quarterbacks. In 2004, he was voted into the Pro Bowl. Brees was also named NFL Comeback Player of the Year, an award given to the player who best overcomes adversity from the previous season.

## Decision Time

Brees excelled in 2004, but he had reached the end of his rookie contract. The Chargers needed to make a decision. Should they sign Brees to a new deal or let him leave for another team and elevate Philip Rivers to the starter's role? Rivers seemed ready, but Brees was still young, and he had just led the Chargers to the playoffs. San Diego decided to stick with Brees, but according to NFL rules, they only needed to offer a one-year deal for $8 million, based on the average salary of the top five quarterbacks in the NFL. Brees agreed to stay with the Chargers for another season.

Based on their record, the Chargers faced a tougher schedule in 2005. They proceeded to drop four of their first five games, even though all the losses were by four points or fewer. San Diego later won five straight but then lost three of their last four to finish 9–7, third in their division and out of the playoffs.

When San Diego fell to the Denver Broncos 23–7 on December 31, 2005, the loss did not just hurt the Chargers. For Drew Brees, the game nearly ended his career.

## Devastating Injury

Late in the second quarter, Drew Brees dove to the ground for a loose ball. Broncos lineman Gerard Warren fell on his right arm, and Brees suffered both a torn labrum and a torn rotator cuff in his

In the last game of the 2005 season, Drew Brees suffered a terrible shoulder injury that threatened his career.

right (throwing) shoulder. Brees had previously separated his left shoulder, but he immediately knew that this injury was much, much worse. He remembers thinking, "Maybe this is the last time I'll ever wear a football uniform. This could be the end of my career. The feeling was … terrifying."

Some doctors thought it unlikely that Brees could return to play at all, while others gave him no more than a 25 percent chance. Brees's surgery was performed by Dr. James Andrews, one of the best orthopedic surgeons in the country. Dr. Andrews specialized in knees, shoulders, and elbows. Brees faced months of intense physical therapy, but people around him knew that if anyone was capable of coming back from such a serious injury, Drew Brees could. Brees's fighting spirit amazed Andrews, who said, "I've never seen an athlete mentally tougher or more motivated."

While Brees rehabilitated his shoulder, another kind of recovery was taking place on the southeastern coast of the United States. This one, however, involved an entire city.

## Katrina's Wrath

On August 29, 2005, Hurricane Katrina came ashore at Plaquemines Parish, Louisiana, approximately 45 miles (70 kilometers) southeast of New Orleans. Packing winds of more than 170 miles (275 km) per hour, Katrina continued to the northeast, accompanied by a storm surge of water more than 26 feet (8 m) high. Katrina's power inundated cities and communities along the coast, including Gulfport and Biloxi, Mississippi.

While Katrina's winds did not hit New Orleans with full force, the city fell victim to a combination of storm surge and more than 10 inches (25 centimeters) of rain. Much of New Orleans lies below

In August 2005, Hurricane Katrina totally destroyed many New Orleans neighborhoods.

sea level, and a system of dikes and levees holds back the waters of Lake Pontchartrain and Lake Borgne located nearby. Katrina's force quickly overwhelmed the city's defenses, and floodwaters raged throughout New Orleans. By late afternoon on August 29, about 20 percent of the city was already underwater. Two days later, more than 80 percent of New Orleans was lost to the flood.

More than one million people evacuated New Orleans and the surrounding area before Katrina arrived, but thousands of other, mostly poorer residents, could not leave in time. Some remained at home, while others took shelter in public buildings, including the Louisiana Superdome and the New Orleans Convention Center. With no national or state relief efforts in place, local police, firefighters, and other service agencies found themselves unable to respond to the growing emergency. Their offices and equipment were also covered by more than 20 feet (6 m) of water.

## Disaster

New Orleans quickly descended into a state of chaos. The city had no electricity, sewers had flooded, roads were blocked, and people faced severe shortages of water and food. Just three days after Katrina, more than fifty thousand people had fled their lawless neighborhoods and moved to the Superdome or the Convention Center. However, both buildings had suffered extensive damage and lacked basic necessities, leaving them unsafe and unhealthy.

It took nearly a week before troops arrived to establish order and distribute food and water. The evacuation of hurricane victims continued, and crews began to rebuild the collapsed levees. On September 6, local police estimated that there were fewer than ten thousand residents left in New Orleans. The last floodwaters were pumped out of the city forty-three days after Katrina arrived.

In the end, Katrina claimed more than 1,800 lives and caused $160 billion in damages. While many residents eventually returned, in 2011, the population of New Orleans was still 29 percent lower than it had been before the hurricane.

## A City Beckons

Drew Brees's one-year contract with San Diego ended after the 2005 season. He was now a free agent, meaning that he could solicit offers from any team in the NFL looking for a new quarterback. Brees initially wanted to stay with the Chargers. Some NFL quarterbacks have managed to spend their entire career with one team, including Troy Aikman with the Dallas Cowboys, John Elway with the Denver Broncos, and Dan Marino with the Miami Dolphins. Brees had originally hoped to do the same with San Diego.

While the Chargers remained interested in retaining Brees, they wondered if he would be able to fully recover from his shoulder injury. They also had Philip Rivers, who was growing impatient and wanted to grab the reins of the Chargers' offense. In the end, San Diego decided to offer less money and security than Brees thought a top quarterback deserved. He decided to field offers from other teams.

Several NFL clubs reached out to Brees. Some viewed him as a backup, but the New Orleans Saints and the Miami Dolphins appeared to want him as their starter. Things initially looked promising with the Dolphins, but their team doctors examined Brees's shoulder and felt he presented too much risk. The Saints,

Thousands of New Orleans residents took shelter in the Louisiana Superdome during Hurricane Katrina. The resulting damage from the hurricane left the stadium unusable for an entire season.

however, had no doubts. They wanted Drew Brees to play quarterback in New Orleans.

## The "Aints"

The New Orleans Saints entered the NFL when the league expanded in 1967. New Orleans was already famous for its great food and music, especially jazz. The Saints took their name from the famous jazz song "When the Saints Go Marching In."

Drew Brees joined the New Orleans Saints as a free agent in 2006 under new head coach Sean Payton (*left*) and General Manager Mickey Loomis (*right*).

Like most expansion teams (teams that are new to the league), the Saints had a rough first year and won only three games. Unfortunately, the Saints continued to struggle for many years, and it took twenty seasons for New Orleans to post their first winning record. Fans began calling their team the "Aints," with some wearing paper bags over their heads while they attended games.

The Saints did feature some notable players during those losing years. One of the most famous was Archie Manning, who played quarterback from 1971 through 1982. Manning twice made the Pro Bowl, and he was widely respected throughout the league, even though the best record he could manage with poor teams was only 8–8. After he retired, Archie Manning remained connected with the community as a resident and supporter of New Orleans. He also gained new fame as his sons, Peyton and Eli Manning, became two of the NFL's top quarterbacks.

## Fleeting Success

In 1987, the Saints finally became a winning team. They did it in a big way, finishing 12–3 and making the playoffs for the first time, before losing to the Minnesota Vikings in the opening round. While New Orleans posted winning records the next two years, they failed to qualify for the postseason. After that, the Saints returned to the playoffs for three consecutive seasons, but each ended with a first-round elimination.

New Orleans then fell back and lost ten or more games each year between 1996 and 1999. After one successful campaign in 2000, which included their first playoff win, New Orleans failed to make another postseason appearance for the next five seasons.

## Starting Fresh

When Hurricane Katrina devastated New Orleans in August 2005, it also left the Superdome, the Saints' home field, unusable for the NFL season due to begin that September. Forced to split their home games between the Louisiana State Tigers' college stadium and San Antonio's Alamo Dome, the Saints suffered through a disastrous year and finished 3–13. Team officials even considered a permanent move to San Antonio or Los Angeles before finally agreeing to stay in New Orleans until at least 2025.

The Saints knew they had to make changes. As a first step, they hired Sean Payton to be their new head coach for 2006. Payton had never headed a team, but he had been a successful assistant coach for nine years in the NFL, mostly as offensive coordinator for the New York Giants and the Dallas Cowboys. Payton wanted to create a high-powered spread offense for his new team, and he needed a great passing quarterback to make it work. Sean Payton wanted Drew Brees.

Drew Brees led the Saints to victory in their first game at the Superdome since Hurricane Katrina.

## Courtship

Payton knew that the combination of Katrina's destruction and the team's past history would make it difficult to attract new players. When he decided to recruit Brees to join the Saints, Payton invited Drew and Brittany to visit New Orleans. Payton hoped to convince them that New Orleans offered more than just the chance to play football. Payton wanted Drew and Brittany to view the team as their extended family and to place their roots in the community.

When Payton did discuss football, he told Brees that he would design plays suited to Brees's talents and that Brees would help shape the offense. Brees also remembers getting the feeling that Payton and the Saints "had more confidence in me and my ability to come back from surgery than I did. That meant a lot."

## Rising Up

In March 2006, Drew Brees signed a contract with the New Orleans Saints for six years and $60 million. Four months after his surgery, Brees was throwing a football again, prompting his doctor to say that Drew's recovery "has been one of the most remarkable of any patient I've ever treated."

When the 2006 NFL season began, Drew Brees, Sean Payton, and the New Orleans Saints were ready. Playing their first two games on the road, the Saints won both. Then, on Monday night, September 25, 2006, the Saints played their home opener in front of a national television audience and a sold-out crowd at the refurbished Superdome. It was the dome's first game since Katrina. When the Saints defeated their division rival the Atlanta Falcons

23–3, the victory stood as a sign that the team, the fans, and the city had started the long path to recovery.

After winning five of their first six games, the Saints overcame a midseason slump to end the regular season as the NFL's most improved team. Their 10–6 record clinched them both the top spot in their division as well as a place in the playoffs. The Saints also went on to beat the Philadelphia Eagles in the first round before losing on the road to the Chicago Bears.

After the game, the Saints traveled back to New Orleans. They did not arrive until around two o'clock the next morning, but thousands of fans showed up at the airport to welcome them home. Brees and the Saints had helped restore a sense of hope and pride to the entire city, and their fans roared their appreciation as the players exited the plane.

Brees had enjoyed an impressive first year in New Orleans. However, the Saints would hit a few more bumps in the road before they would achieve their ultimate prize.

Chapter 4

# Super Performance

When Drew and Brittany Brees first visited New Orleans during free agency, the Saints took them to dinner at a restaurant owned by famous chef Emeril Lagasse. Lagasse later left a cookbook at the table. When Brees opened it, he saw that Emeril had written a message inside the front cover: "Drew: You sign with the Saints, and I'll be cooking your first meal for you in your house here in New Orleans." That was just a taste of the kind of attention and appreciation Drew Brees would find in New Orleans, which would only grow as both he and the team became more successful.

## Gratitude and Awards

Drew Brees's first season in New Orleans had been magical. The team's performance had raised the city's spirits in ways well beyond the playing field, and people expressed their appreciation wherever he appeared in the city. "It's never 'Good game,' or 'Can I have your

*Opposite:* Drew Brees admires his Most Valuable Player trophy after leading New Orleans to victory in the Super Bowl.

autograph?'" Brees said. "It's always somebody saying 'Thank you.' ... I play football for a job. But all this, it goes way beyond football."

In addition to his team's success, Brees also proved that he had totally recovered from his serious shoulder surgery. Sean Payton featured the passing game as he had promised, and Brees responded by leading the NFL with 4,418 passing yards and throwing for 26 touchdowns. Brees was named first team All-Pro, and Sean Payton won NFL Head Coach of the Year. Brees was also proud to be named cowinner of the Walter Payton NFL Man of the Year award, in recognition of his extensive charity work in New Orleans.

Things appeared to be looking up for Brees and the Saints. Over the next two years, however, Drew Brees would face more adversity, both professionally and personally.

## A Step Back

Each NFL season brings new challenges. The 2006 Saints had been assembled from many pieces, and they had gone on to experience a storybook season. Now came the hard part; they had to prove that 2006 had not been a fluke by repeating their success and continuing the rebuilding effort that had started the year before.

Facing a much stronger schedule in 2007, the Saints opened the season against the Super Bowl champion Indianapolis Colts. The Saints had missed playing the Colts for the Super Bowl title by one game the previous season, so they were looking forward to testing themselves against the league's best team.

It did not take long for the Saints to realize that 2007 would be very different than 2006. New Orleans ended the first half tied at 10–10, but the Colts surged after halftime and blew out the Saints, 41–10. Brees said afterwards that the Saints felt "humiliated" after the loss. He was sure they would turn things around in their second game against the Tampa Bay Buccaneers. He was wrong.

The Saints lost big to the Buccaneers, 31–14, and then they dropped their third game by the same score. When New Orleans then fell to the Carolina Panthers, their season record stood at 0–4. While the Saints managed to win their next four games, Brees and his team then faltered. They ended the season with more losses than wins.

This Green Bay Packers fan wears a paper bag with the word "AINTS" to mock the Saints and their fans. Saints fans often covered their faces with paper bags due to the team's poor record before Drew Brees arrived in New Orleans.

## More Disappointment

Brees and the Saints fared no better in 2008, ending with an 8–8 record and once again missing the playoffs. Even so, Saints fans watched Brees direct an exciting offense as he passed for 34 touchdowns and a league-leading 5,069 yards. Brees became only the second quarterback at the time to throw for more than 5,000 yards in one season. Brees also made the Pro Bowl and was named Offensive Player of the Year.

In his 2010 book, *Coming Back Stronger*, Brees remembers 2007 and 2008 as difficult seasons. He felt that he and his teammates learned valuable lessons, however, which helped fuel their huge turnaround the following year and prepared them to earn football's ultimate prize.

## Joy and Sadness

The new year started great for Drew and Brittany Brees. On January 15, 2009, Drew's thirtieth birthday, the couple celebrated the birth of their first child, Baylen Robert Brees. Little did they know how famous Baylen and his father would become just a little more than one year later.

Drew and Brittany would have three more children as of 2019. Their second son, Bowen Christopher Brees, was born on October 19, 2010. Their third son, Callen Christian Brees, was born on August 15, 2012. Their daughter, Rylen Judith Brees, was born on August, 25, 2014.

Life turned much darker for Brees during the Saints' summer training camp. On August 7, 2009, Brees received news that his mother, Mina, had suddenly passed away from a prescription drug overdose. Her death was ruled a suicide, and she left behind written notes for several people, including Drew, his brother Reid, and Drew's newborn son, Baylen.

## Feelings of Regret

Brees describes his mother as a person who was strongly focused on getting her own way, no matter how it affected other people, including her children. After Brees's parents divorced, Mina had become a successful attorney and political leader in Austin. Over the years, however, Brees's relationship with his mother deteriorated.

Brees eventually came to believe that his mother may have been suffering from mental illness that contributed to her mood swings and controlling behavior. He hoped to mend their differences, and he thought that the birth of his son Baylen might help them grow closer after so many years apart.

After Mina's death, Brees discovered that his mother had been struggling with prescription drug abuse for many years. He wondered if he would have been able to help if he had known more about what she had been going through. Brees credits his family and his faith with helping him get through that difficult time.

## Full Commitment

Brees and the Saints entered the 2009 season determined to correct the weaknesses that sabotaged their efforts the previous two seasons. They adopted the phrase "finish strong" as one of their main themes for the year. The Saints had something to prove, both to their fans and to themselves.

Everyone knew that New Orleans already had one of the best offenses in the league, but coach Sean Payton realized that he needed better performance on the other side of the line. Payton hired a new defensive coordinator, Gregg Williams, to install a more aggressive and effective system and match what the Saints already had on offense.

## Impressive Start

The Saints opened their 2009 season by crushing the Detroit Lions, 45–27, with Brees throwing six touchdown passes. New Orleans then beat the Philadelphia Eagles by an even wider margin the following week, 48–22. After their first five games, the Saints stood 5–0, outscoring their opponents by an average of twenty points.

Over the next three months, the Saints ran the table by winning their first thirteen games. The streak looked like it might end in game seven against the Miami Dolphins. The Saints fell behind, 24–3, but Drew Brees led a huge comeback, and he ran for the game-winning touchdown in a 46–34 victory. The Saints cooled off a bit after that, losing their next two games. By that point, however, they had already clinched the top spot in the playoffs. Sean Payton decided to rest his key players in the last game of the season in order to best prepare for a Super Bowl run.

## Two Big Wins

The Saints finished the regular season 13–3, featuring one of the greatest offenses in NFL history. Drew Brees set an NFL record for completion percentage (70.6 percent) and led all quarterbacks in touchdown passes (34), passing yards (4,388 yards), and quarterback rating (109.6), which is a measure of quarterback efficiency. Brees became so popular that he even filmed a commercial with President Barack Obama at the White House.

The Saints now needed to win two playoff games. In the first, New Orleans soundly defeated the Arizona Cardinals 45–14, and Drew Brees completed 23 passes in 32 attempts for 247 yards, 3 touchdowns, and no interceptions. The Saints would now face off against the Minnesota Vikings for the chance to go to Miami and play in the Super Bowl.

## Overtime Thriller

On January 24, 2010, the Saints and Vikings engaged in an intense, back-and-forth battle that would not be decided until overtime.

Minnesota scored first, but Brees quickly answered back, passing thirty-eight yards to running back Pierre Thomas to tie the score. After Vikings quarterback Brett Favre threw his own touchdown pass, Brees again responded by throwing a nine-yarder, and the teams reached halftime knotted at 14–14.

When the second half began, the Saints and Vikings repeated the same pattern, only in reverse. Drew Brees led his team to two touchdowns, but the Vikings countered each time. The fourth quarter ended with the teams tied 28–28. Overtime loomed, and the team that scored first would cash its ticket to play for the championship trophy.

## Super Drive

The Saints won the overtime coin toss and chose to receive the ball. Pierre Thomas returned the kickoff forty yards. Drew Brees then went to work, driving his team all the way to the Vikings' twenty-two yard line. First-year kicker Garrett Hartley then kicked a field goal to give the Saints a 31–28 victory. The Saints were on their way to Florida and their first Super Bowl appearance in franchise history.

## Championship Fever

Excitement had been growing among Saints fans ever since Drew Brees arrived in New Orleans. Saints lovers had started to gather at the airport after away games, lining the half-mile road between the airline terminal and the highway to welcome their Saints back home, win or lose. Treating each return like one big party, fans brought food and drinks and blared loud music while they cheered Saints players who drove by.

By 2009, the number of fans coming to the airport had grown to as many as thirty thousand, and Brees remembers that it sometimes took nearly ninety minutes to travel through the crowd. Each trip resembled a parade, with fans surrounding the cars, reaching for autographs, and touching the players. The police eventually set up barricades along the route to keep everyone safe.

Saints fans now hoped that their beloved team could complete their mission and bring a Super Bowl championship back to New Orleans.

## An American Tradition

Before 1966, two different football leagues, the NFL and the American Football League (AFL), held their own separate championships. After agreeing to merge, their respective champions began to play each other for the overall title.

The NFL now includes two conferences, the American Football Conference (AFC) and the National Football Conference (NFC). Each year, on the first Sunday in February, the winner of each conference plays for the NFL championship in the Super Bowl. The game's location changes each season. Since the Super Bowl takes place early in the calendar year after the NFL season ends, the NFL uses Roman numerals to eliminate confusion. Over time, Super Bowl Sunday evolved into an unofficial American holiday, attracting more television viewers each year than any other program.

On February 7, 2010, the New Orleans Saints and the Indianapolis Colts faced off against each other in Sun Life Stadium in Miami Gardens, Florida, in Super Bowl XLIV, the forty-fourth Super Bowl.

## Big Day, Slow Start

The Saints took the field as underdogs against the Colts. Peyton Manning, one of the NFL's greatest all-time quarterbacks, had led the Colts to first place in their division with a record of fourteen wins and only two losses. The Colts then charged through the AFC playoffs, soundly defeating the Baltimore Ravens (20–3) and the New York Jets (30–17). During his career, Peyton Manning had already won one Super Bowl and four NFL MVP awards.

Drew Brees was prepared, but he admits he still felt butterflies as the game began. New Orleans received the ball first but had to give up the ball to the Colts after only three plays. Manning immediately drove the Colts down the field for a field goal and a 3–0 lead. After the Saints again failed to move the ball, Manning led another drive, finishing with a touchdown pass to wide receiver Pierre Garçon just as the first quarter ended. In the biggest game of Drew Brees's life, Peyton Manning and the Indianapolis Colts had jumped to a 10–0 lead.

Quarterback Drew Brees (#9) throws a touchdown pass to tight end Jeremy Shockey (#88) in Super Bowl XLIV.

## Coming Back

Refusing to panic, Drew Brees and his offense finally started to get into a rhythm in the second quarter and managed to put two field goals on the board. Although the Saints had largely been outplayed so far, they only trailed the Colts 10–6 at halftime.

When the third quarter began, New Orleans was set to kick the ball to the Colts offense. Coach Sean Payton had other plans, however. Instead of doing what everyone expected, Payton made a very unusual decision to try and take control of the game and get Drew Brees back on the field. Rather than kick off like everyone expected, Payton called for an onside kick.

## Huge Gamble

Sean Payton had the reputation of never being afraid to call aggressive plays when needed. According to Brees, Payton had been talking about an onside kick all week. The play involves kicking the ball only a short distance and then trying to recover it for your own team. However, onside kicks come with a great deal of risk. If the other team recovers, they have the ball in very good field position, with a great chance to score.

Kicking teams rarely recover an onside kick, and coaches usually call that play only when they are desperate, trailing at the end of a game with little time left to score. It would be very unusual to call an onside kick to start the second half, especially since this was such an important game, and the Saints were down by only four points. However, Sean Payton wanted to shake things up and surprise the Colts, so he rolled the dice.

# Praises On and Off the Field

When Drew Brees led the New Orleans Saints to victory in Super Bowl XLIV, his former college coach expected nothing less. "I don't want to suggest I had a crystal ball," Joe Tiller said, "but nothing Drew does surprised me. He's very talented ... Not only has Drew matured into a real field general, but he's with a coach who knows what his strengths are. The system complements him perfectly."

While everyone praised Brees for his on-field exploits, many also noted that Drew Brees's influence extended far beyond football. Former Westlake High School teammate Matt Matza once said that Brees was "a better human being maybe than a football player, and he's a great football player, but he's just such a great individual." New Orleans running back Mark Ingram echoed those sentiments, telling *Sporting News*, "Everyone knows he is a great football player, but he's also a great guy—fun to be around, very down to earth, and doesn't think he is better than anyone else."

Mark Brunell had himself been a Pro Bowl quarterback before serving as Brees's backup during the Super Bowl year. In his foreword for Brees's book, *Coming Back Stronger*, Brunell wrote, "I can honestly say that Drew Brees is a champion in every sense of the word ... That passion is by no means limited to the football field. His commitment to his family, his friends, and the kids and communities he supports is positively unmatched."

## Taking Charge

The play shocked everyone as it unfolded, including the Colts, and the Saints successfully recovered the onside kick. Brees now had the ball in great field position. After setting up the Colts defense with some short passes and runs, Brees hit running back Pierre Thomas with a sixteen-yard touchdown pass. New Orleans had taken their first lead of the game, 13–10.

The Colts responded quickly, with Peyton Manning driving his team the length of the field to regain the lead, 17–13. The Saints countered with a field goal near the end of the third quarter to make the score 17–16. The Colts now led the Saints by a single point, and one final fifteen-minute quarter would decide the NFL championship.

## Holding On

The Colts' first drive of the fourth quarter ended with a missed field goal. With about ten minutes left, Brees completed six straight passes to drive the Saints close to the goal line. Brees then flipped a short pass to tight end Jeremy Shockey, who charged into the end zone.

The Saints now held the lead, 22–17. Kicking the extra point would put them ahead by six, meaning that Peyton Manning and the Colts could still win the game with a touchdown and an extra point. Sean Payton decided to take another gamble.

Rather than kick for one point, New Orleans tried for a two-point conversion. A two-point conversion is when the scoring team has the option to add two additional points by running or passing the ball into the end zone on one play starting from the opponent's two-yard line. Brees passed to receiver Lance Moore,

Brees raises his son Baylen into the air after Super Bowl XLIV as his wife, Brittany (*right*), looks on. Baylen wore headphones on the field to shield him from the noise.

and after catching the ball, Moore extended his arms toward the goal line. The ball was knocked loose as Moore hit the ground, and an official ruled the pass incomplete. The Saints believed that Moore had scored before the ball came loose, however, and they challenged the call on the field. The referee reviewed the play and overturned the call, awarding the Saints the two points. New Orleans now led 24–17.

## Frantic Finish

The Colts were not done. Peyton Manning took the ball with fewer than six minutes left and drove his team all the way to the Saints' thirty-one-yard line. Manning then targeted wide receiver Reggie Wayne, but New Orleans defensive back Tracy Porter intercepted the pass and ran it back seventy-four yards for a Saints touchdown, all but clinching the victory.

Brees didn't see Porter's interception as it happened; he was planning his next offensive series in case the Colts scored. Brees only looked up when he heard the crowd roar, and he saw Porter running toward the end zone. The touchdown extended lead for the Saints to 31–17.

When the Saints defense stopped the Colts on the five-yard line with forty-four seconds to go, Brees ran out on the field to run one more play and clinch the win. Brees crouched down behind his offensive line, received the ball, and knelt down. The clock ticked down, and the game was over.

The days of Saints fans calling themselves the "Aints" and covering their faces with paper bags were finally over. Drew Brees and the New Orleans Saints had finally won the Super Bowl.

Winning Saints quarterback Drew Brees triumphantly displays the Super Bowl trophy to the crowd.

9
NFL
Reebok

9
NFL
28
SAINTS

Chapter 5

# Still Building His Legacy

About 106 million people watched Super Bowl XLIV on television, the largest United States audience for any program at the time. Brees received many accolades and awards, including game MVP. What he treasured most, however, was celebrating the win on the field and holding his son Baylen high above his head as colorful confetti fell from the sky.

New Orleans had already been preparing for its famous Mardi Gras celebration, so the city was poised to honor the Saints with a joyful victory parade the following Tuesday. Close to one million people turned out to cheer, as Saints players, coaches, and staff members threw beads from floats rolling along the city's streets. New Orleans finally had a winner and something to celebrate after years of suffering due to Hurricane Katrina.

Drew Brees reached the pinnacle of professional success by winning Super Bowl XLIV. However, he was far from done. Brees continues to accomplish great things, both as a player and in the community.

*Opposite:* Drew and Brittany Brees are shown here with their sons, (*left to right*) Baylen, Callen, and Bowen, and their daughter, Rylen.

## No Repeat

The New Orleans Saints began the 2010 season eager to defend their Super Bowl title. After winning their first two games, they went 2–3 before winning their next six to finish 11–5. The Atlanta Falcons had an even better year, though, winning the division by two games. The Saints made the playoffs, so they traveled to Seattle to play the Seahawks.

Seattle had become the first team in NFL history to qualify for the postseason with a losing record, finishing with nine losses against only seven wins. Most experts picked the Saints to win. Brees passed for two touchdowns, but the underdog Seahawks eliminated the Saints in a huge upset, 41–36.

The Saints then went 13–3 the next season and made the playoffs once again. After defeating the Detroit Lions in the first round, however, the Saints lost to the San Francisco 49ers. That summer, Brees and the Saints agreed on a new five-year contract for a then-record $100 million.

## Scandal

The 2012 season began under a dark cloud. The NFL accused the Saints of paying bonuses to their defense for dishing out especially violent hits on opposing players and even intentionally injuring them. Not only did these actions violate NFL rules and demonstrate poor sportsmanship, they were also dangerous. Drew Brees denied involvement and felt that the NFL didn't have clear evidence, but the league still suspended coach Sean Payton for the entire 2012 season.

Payton's absence and a negative atmosphere helped ruin the Saints' season before it even started. Brees still threw for more than

5,000 yards and 43 touchdowns, but the Saints finished 7–9 and missed the playoffs for the first time in four years.

## Good and Bad

Sean Payton returned as head coach in 2013, and the Saints bounced back with an 11–5 record, but a loss in their second playoff game left them short of reaching the Super Bowl. For the next three years, Brees continued to direct one of the league's best offenses, but the defense could not keep up. New Orleans posted three consecutive 7–9 records from 2014 to 2016.

In 2017, the Saints returned to their winning ways with a stronger effort, collecting eleven victories and a division title. New Orleans then won its first playoff game before losing the next in shocking fashion. As the time clock expired, the Minnesota Vikings came from behind to complete a touchdown pass of sixty-one yards that won the game, sending the Saints home short of their goal.

## Handled with Class

On March 13, 2018, Brees signed a new two-year contract extension worth $50 million with the Saints. He then proceeded to break Peyton Manning's all-time record for passing yards and the NFL record for completion percentage, leading the Saints to thirteen wins and another first-place finish in the division.

However, the team's postseason once again ended suddenly, one game away from another Super Bowl appearance. With fewer than two minutes remaining against the Los Angeles Rams, a controversial missed penalty call stopped New Orleans from clinching what appeared to be certain victory. The Rams won in overtime, and many New Orleans fans reacted bitterly. Showing the

Drew Brees set a new NFL record for all-time passing yardage in October 2018.

professionalism he had always been known for, Drew Brees refused to blame the loss on that one play. Brees explained, "Regardless of the call or no call, I felt like there were other opportunities for us that I wish we could've taken advantage of."

## One of the Greatest

Drew Brees showed no signs of slowing down as he prepared for yet another season in 2019. Brees had risen to become one of the greatest quarterbacks in NFL history, and he now holds some of football's most prestigious all-time records.

Drew Brees's influence off the field may even be bigger than what he has accomplished playing football. Brees continues to devote much of his personal time to improving the lives of others through his charitable foundation and his involvement in many other community activities.

## Man of Faith

Drew Brees has stated publicly that he is proud to be a Christian, and his faith directs him in his daily life. Brees remembers that when he injured his knee in high school, his church pastor mentioned that God was looking for a "few good men" to use their skills to make things better for others, and Brees decided that he wanted to follow that same path.

Brees also saw other athletes become heavily involved in charity work, and he thought that many of them seemed to have experienced hardship in their own lives that motivated them to help others. He believes that he has been given many gifts, and he now has a responsibility to use his position to help others.

## Started in College

Brees began to devote much of his time to charitable causes when he entered Purdue University. In addition to attending classes and playing football, Brees worked with many local organizations, especially those that helped improve the lives of children and their families. His work with school-age children led a second-grade teacher to praise Brees for "his positive influence on her students and his willingness to work with them one-on-one." She added that Brees had a heart "bigger than the state of Texas."

Brees graduated college in 2001, but he remains involved in the local community of West Lafayette, Indiana, Purdue's home. He sponsors an annual golf tournament there to raise money to help youth in need, and his family donated $2 million to Purdue's academic center.

## Working Together

After they married, Drew and Brittany Brees agreed to make a strong commitment to get even more involved in improving the lives of others. In 2003, they formed the Brees Dream Foundation. Brittany's aunt, Judith Zopp, had struggled valiantly against cancer before succumbing in 2000. Her life inspired Drew and Brittany to begin their foundation by supporting cancer research and helping those who already had the disease, especially children. All the money that their foundation raises goes back into that same community to help the people in the area.

Brees's commitment to getting involved in cancer research led to his friendship with Micah Roshell, a young boy from New Orleans who had been struggling with cancer. After New Orleans defeated the Arizona Cardinals in the 2010 playoffs, Brees visited the hospital and gave Micah the game ball.

## Rebuilding New Orleans

When Brees joined the Saints as a free agent in 2006, he and Brittany wasted no time in joining the New Orleans community that was still struggling less than one year after Katrina. The couple bought an older home in New Orleans that needed a lot of work. They spent

# Twenty-Five Years of Leadership

Drew Brees began racking up awards while still in high school. He led his Westlake varsity team to undefeated seasons and the Texas state championship, and he was also chosen as the title game's MVP.

Brees continued his exemplarily performance in college at Purdue University, quarterbacking the Boilermakers to their first Rose Bowl appearance in more than thirty years. Brees twice was named Big Ten Player of Year, and he graduated college as the conference's all-time leader in passing yards, completions, and completion percentage.

Beyond the playing field, Brees was named Academic All-American Player of Year and won Purdue's Leonard Wilson Award for unselfishness and dedication. He also won the first-ever Socrates Award, recognizing the nation's finest athlete in terms of academics, athletics, and community service.

Still going strong after more than eighteen years in the NFL, Drew Brees stands out as one of the greatest professional quarterbacks of all time. As of 2019, Brees ranks number one in career pass completions, passing yards, and completion percentage, and number two in passing touchdowns. Brees has been named to twelve Pro Bowls as of 2019, and he was awarded the NFL Comeback Player of the Year in 2004, the Walter Payton Man of the Year in 2006, and the Offensive Player of the Year in 2008 and 2011. Perhaps most importantly, Brees won the Super Bowl Most Valuable Player Award after the 2009 season.

Drew Brees continues to help rebuild the New Orleans community through charities, including Habitat for Humanity.

two years fixing and renovating the house, but they felt that it was worth it, in part because it demonstrated to the city and its people that the Brees family was not just there to play football. Drew Brees and his wife were not just dedicated to helping rebuild the New Orleans Saints; they wanted to help the entire city.

Brees had seen some of Katrina's devastation during his visit with Sean Payton; he toured the city again shortly after he signed his contract. Brees told Bob McManaman of the *Arizona Republic,*

"When I visited New Orleans, I saw an opportunity. I felt like it was a calling for me. Not only to come here and turn the organization around … but to help with the rebuilding of a city and a region." Brees quickly began raising money to aid the rebuilding efforts.

## Kids, Schools, and Sports

Upon establishing themselves in New Orleans, Drew and Brittany wondered where to start their charitable work. So much needed to be done. They learned that many residents forced to leave the city had not yet been able to return. Drew and Brittany decided to focus their efforts on helping residents move back into their neighborhoods. They thought that supporting schools and sports programs would help, so they targeted education, parks, athletics, and other activities that included children.

After taking a year to assess where they might be able to do the most good, Drew and Brittany partnered with Operation Kids to launch the Rebuilding Dreams in New Orleans campaign. By May 2009, they had raised $1.8 million in funding to support twelve organizations devoted to that purpose, including schools, arts programs, and recreational areas. Later, the Brees Dream Foundation raised millions of dollars to help rebuild schools and athletic fields. Successful projects included a new football stadium for the Ninth Ward public schools, an area that had been particularly devastated by Katrina.

The hurricane had also destroyed the entire athletic center at Lusher Charter School. Brees's Rebuilding Dreams charity raised $671,000 to rebuild the center. Brees also launched the Quarterback Club, which brought together some of the city's wealthiest citizens to lead special projects. These influential people helped raise

$2 million for the Katrina relief effort, including money used for the New Orleans Ballet Association and the rebuilding of a stadium at City Park.

## National Recognition

Other projects supported by the Brees Dream Foundation include feeding hungry families, helping teenagers learn healthy life habits, and challenging children to put their creative ideas into action. In 2010, Brees made a video to support the antibullying campaign It Gets Better, telling kids, "If you're making fun of someone because they're different, then you are no friend of mine."

Drew Brees's charitable work attracted the attention of President Barack Obama, who appointed him cochair of the President's Council on Fitness, Sports, and Nutrition.

The Brees Dream Foundation has contributed more than $25 million to charitable causes. Brees gained so much attention for his work that, in 2010, President Barack Obama appointed him and gymnast Dominique Dawes as cochairs of the President's Council on Fitness, Sports, and Nutrition, which helps Americans become healthy through exercise and diet.

Jon Stinchcombe helped protect Drew Brees as a Saints offensive lineman during their Super Bowl run. Speaking about Brees, Stinchcombe said:

> Not only was he gifted and talented to be one of the best quarterbacks to ever play the game, but he's one of the most positive influences on the city of New Orleans post Katrina … The times that I've seen him go out of his way to change somebody's world … That's the legacy that I think he leaves that far exceeds what he's done with number nine on his chest and a helmet on his head.

Drew Brees continues to lead, whether it means quarterbacking his team on the football field or raising money to improve the lives of people living in New Orleans and around the country. In his book, *Coming Back Stronger*, Brees writes, "Finish strong. It is not where you start in life, but rather how you finish. It's that last play that can make all the difference in the outcome." Drew Brees is nowhere near finished as he continues to make a difference on and off the field.

# Timeline

**January 15, 1979** Drew Brees is born in Texas.

**December 7, 1996** Brees quarterbacks Westlake High School to the Texas state championship, capping an undefeated season.

**August 30, 1998** Brees starts his first college game as quarterback for Purdue University.

**January 1, 2001** Brees and his Purdue Boilermakers play in the Rose Bowl.

**April 21, 2001** The San Diego Chargers select Brees in the NFL draft.

**September 8, 2002** Brees starts his first NFL game.

**February 8, 2003** Brees marries Brittany Dudchenko; later that year, they form the Brees Dream Foundation.

**January 8, 2005** Brees and the Chargers make the playoffs but lose to the New York Jets in overtime.

**August 29, 2005** Hurricane Katrina hits the Gulf Coast and devastates New Orleans.

**December 31, 2005** Brees hurts his right shoulder in the season's final game, jeopardizing his career.

**March 14, 2006** Brees signs with the New Orleans Saints as a free agent.

**December 28, 2008** Brees passes for more than 5,000 yards in a season for the first time.

**January 15, 2009** Baylen Robert Brees is born on Drew Brees's birthday.

**February 7, 2010** Drew Brees leads the Saints to their first Super Bowl championship.

**October 19, 2010** Bowen Christopher Brees is born.

**August 15, 2012** Callen Christian Brees is born; later that year, Brees signs a five-year contract with the Saints worth $100 million.

**August 25, 2014** Rylen Judith Brees is born.

**March 13, 2018** Brees signs a two-year extension to stay with the Saints.

**October 8, 2018** Brees becomes the NFL all-time leader in career passing yards.

**January 20, 2019** Brees and the Saints miss going to another Super Bowl after a controversial overtime loss to the Los Angeles Rams.

# Glossary

**adversity** Challenges or difficulties that people face.

**All-American** A player who is voted as one of the best in the country at his or her position in high school or college.

**All-Pro** An NFL player voted at the end of the season to be the best in the league at his position.

**bowl game** A college football game between two top teams that is held after the regular season.

**comeback** A game that is won by a team that was behind in the score.

**completion** A football pass that is caught by a receiver.

**conference** An organized division of athletic teams within a larger group.

**contract** A legal agreement between a player and a team that defines terms of employment and payments.

**draft** The process by which NFL teams choose players who are leaving college to turn professional.

**foundation** An organization that provides money and support to causes.

**free agent** A player who has no contract and is free to sign with another team.

**Heisman Trophy** An award given each year to the best college football player; considered to be the most prestigious college athletic award.

**interception** A football pass that is caught by a player from the opposing team.

**legacy** A person's long-term influence and contributions.

**overtime** Extra playing time if a game ends in a tie.

**physical therapy** The process of using equipment and exercise to heal various injuries.

**pinnacle** The most successful or highest point.

**playoffs** A series of games that take place after the regular season to determine which teams play for the championship.

**prestigious** Respected and having high status.

**Pro Bowl** The NFL all-star game.

**quarter** One of the four fifteen-minute periods an NFL game is divided into.

**quarterback** A football player in charge of the offense.

**Roman numeral** An ancient Roman system that uses letters to represent numbers. For example, V represents 5, X represents 10, and L represents 50.

**rookie** A first-year participant in a major sport.

**running back** A football player who catches and runs with the ball.

**scholarship** Money that is given to a student by a high school or college to pay for tuition and other expenses, often as a reward for academic or athletic accomplishments.

**tight end** An offensive football player who lines up close to the tackle and plays in a way that is a hybrid of lineman and receiver.

**touchdown** A score in footbal that is made by carrying the ball over the opponent's goal line or by catching the ball while standing in the end zone. Teams can then kick the ball through the goalpost for one additional point or run a play over the goal line for two additional points.

**upset** An unexpected result or situation, especially in a sports competition.

# Further Information

## Books

Aretha, David. *Top 10 Quarterbacks in Football* (Sports Greats). New York, NY: Enslow Publishing, 2017.

Brees, Drew, with Chris Fabry. *Coming Back Stronger: Unleashing the Hidden Power of Adversity.* Carol Stream, IL: Tyndale House Publishers, 2010.

Geoffreys, Clayton. *Drew Brees: The Inspiring Story of One of Football's Most Resilient Quarterbacks* (Football Biography Books). Winter Park, FL: Calvintir Books, LLC, 2017.

Payton, Sean. *Home Team: Coaching the Saints and New Orleans Back to Life.* New York, NY: New American Library, 2010.

Rivlin, Gary. *Katrina: After the Flood.* New York, NY: Simon & Schuster Paperbacks, 2015.

## Websites

### The Brees Dream Foundation

http://www.drewbrees.com
Drew and Brittany Brees founded their charitable foundation in 2003. The website includes descriptions and videos of foundation events as well as information about Brees and his life.

## Drew Brees Stats

https://www.pro-football-reference.com/players/B/BreeDr00.htm
This webpage lists all of Drew Brees's professional career statistics.

## Hurricane Katrina

https://www.nationalgeographic.com/environment/natural-disasters/reference/hurricane-katrina
This National Geographic website tells the story of Hurricane Katrina in words and pictures, including how the storm's effects are still felt today in New Orleans and on the Gulf Coast.

## Key Moments in Saints History

https://www.neworleanssaints.com/team/history/key-moments
The website lists every important moment in New Orleans Saints history, year by year, from the team's beginning through the current year.

## New Orleans Saints

http://www.nfl.com/teams/neworleanssaints/profile?team=NO
NFL.com includes separate pages for each NFL team with news, statistics, and video highlights. Featured here is the page for the Saints.

# Videos

## Drew Brees Breaks All-Time Passing Yards Record

https://www.youtube.com/watch?v=XXqXHPT4aMw
In 2018, Brees broke Peyton Manning's record for all-time passing yards. This video shows the play that set the new record as well as the on-field celebration, including Brees meeting his family on the sidelines.

## Super Bowl XLIV: Saints vs. Colts Highlights

https://www.youtube.com/watch?v=P0zuCOfcSjc
Watch video highlights of Drew Brees and the New Orleans Saints defeating Peyton Manning and the Indianapolis Colts in Super Bowl XLIV.

# Bibliography

Allen, Kathy. *Drew Brees* (Football Stars Up Close). New York, NY: Bearport Publishing, 2013.

Augustyn, Adam. "New Orleans Saints: American Football Team." Britannica, January 23, 2019. https://www.britannica.com/topic/New-Orleans-Saints.

Boehler, Adam, and Sabrina Crewe. *Drew Brees* (Superstars!). New York, NY: Crabtree Publishing Company, 2013.

Brees, Drew, with Chris Fabry. *Coming Back Stronger: Unleashing the Hidden Power of Adversity.* Carol Stream, IL: Tyndale House Publishers, 2010.

"Brees Wants No Part of Mom's Campaign in Texas." ESPN.com, October 31, 2016. http://www.espn.com/nfl/news/story?id=2644387.

Christopher, Matt. *Drew Brees* (Great Americans in Sports). New York, NY: Little, Brown and Company, 2015.

DiPrimio, Pete. *Drew Brees* (Blue Banner Biography). Hockessin, DE: Mitchell Lane Publishers, 2011.

"Doug Flutie." Britannica, October 19, 2018. https://www.britannica.com/biography/Doug-Flutie.

"Drew Brees." NewOrleansSaints.com. Accessed March 5, 2019. https://www.neworleanssaints.com/team/players-roster/drew-brees/.

"Drew Brees." ProFootballReference.com. Accessed March 2, 2019. https://www.pro-football-reference.com/players/B/BreeDr00.htm.

"Drew Brees." SportsReference.com. Accessed March 4, 2019. https://www.sports-reference.com/cfb/players/drew-brees-1.html.

"Drew's Bio." DrewBrees.com. Accessed February 27, 2019. http://www.drewbrees.com/drews-bio/.

Eisenberg, Jeff. "The Tough Break That Enabled Drew Brees' Rise to Stardom." Yahoo Sports, October 8, 2018. https://sports.yahoo.com/tough-break-enabled-drew-brees-rise-stardom-130015418.html.

"40 Quotes for Drew Brees' 40th Birthday." NewOrleansSaints.com. Accessed March 6, 2019. https://www.neworleanssaints.com/photos/40-quotes-for-drew-brees-40th-birthday#897c2624-e515-4438-bfec-5be1d579272e.

Gitlin, Marty. *Drew Brees: Super Bowl Champ* (Playmakers). Edina, MN: ABDO Publishing Company, 2011.

Hlavaty, Craig. "Fascinating Facts About High School Football in Texas." *Houston Chronicle*, August 15, 2018. https://www.houstonchronicle.com/sports/highschool/article/Things-to-know-about-high-school-football-in-Texas-9193558.php#photo-7446686.

"Hurricane Katrina." Britannica, August 16, 2018. https://www.britannica.com/biography/Doug-Flutie.

Kercheval, Ben. "Joe Tiller, All-Time Winningest Coach at Purdue, Dies at 74." CBSSports.com, September 20, 2017.

https://www.cbssports.com/college-football/news/all-time-winningest-coach-at-purdue-joe-tiller-dies-at-74/.

"Key Moments in Saints History." NewOrleansSaints.com. Accessed February 16, 2019. https://www.neworleanssaints.com/team/history/key-moments.

Payton, Sean. *Home Team: Coaching the Saints and New Orleans Back to Life.* New York, NY: New American Library, 2010.

"Peyton Manning Biography." Biography.com, April 27, 2017. https://www.biography.com/people/peyton-manning-37880.

"Purdue Boilermakers School History." SportsReference.com. Accessed March 1, 2019. https://www.sports-reference.com/cfb/schools/purdue/index.html.

Savage, Jeff. *Drew Brees* (Amazing Athletes). Minneapolis, MN: Lerner Publications Company, 2011.

# Index

Page numbers in **boldface** are images.

# About the Author

**Gerry Boehme** is a published author, editor, speaker, and business consultant who loves to travel and learn about new things. He especially enjoys talking with people who have different backgrounds and opinions. Boehme has written books for students dealing with many subjects, including *John Lewis and Desegregation*, *Roberto Clemente: The Pride of Puerto Rico*, and *Serena Williams: Setting New Standards*. He has also spoken at conferences across the United States as well as in the United Kingdom, Australia, and the Republic of Korea. Boehme graduated from the Newhouse School at Syracuse University and lives on Long Island, New York, with his wife and two children. He still celebrates the four Super Bowl championships won by his beloved New York Giants.

CAREERS in Your Community™

# WORKING as a LEGAL ADVOCATE

Janet Harvey

Rosen YA™
New York

Published in 2019 by The Rosen Publishing Group, Inc.
29 East 21st Street, New York, NY 10010



First Edition



**Library of Congress Cataloging-in-Publication Data**

Names: Harvey, Janet (Writer of legal advocacy), author.
Title: Working as a legal advocate / Janet Harvey.
Description: First edition. | New York : Rosen Publishing, 2019. | Series: Careers in your community | Includes bibliographical references and index. | Audience: Grades 7–12.
Identifiers: LCCN 2018013423| ISBN 9781499467277 (library bound) | ISBN 9781499467352 (pbk.)
Subjects: LCSH: Practice of law—Vocational guidance—United States—Juvenile literature. | Law—Vocational guidance—United States—Juvenile literature.
Classification: LCC KF297 .H337 2018 | DDC 340.023/73—dc23
LC record available at https://lccn.loc.gov/2018013423

*Manufactured in the United States of America*